HONORING THE EARTH

HONORING
THE ☙ EARTH

A JOURNAL

OF NEW

EARTH PRAYERS

Elizabeth Roberts and Elias Amidon

HarperSanFrancisco
A Division of HarperCollins *Publishers*

HarperSanFrancisco and the authors, in association with the Rainforest Action Network, will facilitate the planting of two trees for every one tree used in the manufacture of this book.

ISBN 0–06–250738–9

93 94 95 96 97 ❖ HAD 10 9 8 7 6 5 4 3 2

This edition is printed on acid-free paper that meets the American National Standards Institute Z39.48 Standard.

INTRODUCTION

❧

This nearly empty book awaits you like a friend. It waits for you to share what is on your mind and in your heart. Like a friend, this book will accept whatever you say to it. It will reflect back what you most need to hear. It will not tire of you if you want to talk late into the night, and it will not be hurt if you ignore it for months at a time. Each time you open it, it will offer an intimacy and depth far removed from the everyday world of acquaintances and business.

As you turn its pages you will see this book has voices in it already, voices praying by your side, voices reminding you of how you, too, have felt:

> Touch the earth and listen to the rocks
>> for they remember
> They know and remember
>> all that has come to pass here.[1]

These are voices of your sisters and brothers. They speak from China and from Nairobi, from Christianity and from Islam, from cities and from tribes, from the past and from the present. The simple, familiar quality they hold in common we call Earth prayer. *These are the voices of the Earth praying, not in supplication to a distant diety but in recognition of the spirit immanent in* this *world. That spirit interconnects us all, as surely as biology does. At the heart of a life grounded in Earth prayer is this sense of* belonging *with all of creation. Earth prayer is a familiar and unpretentious call of our mutual belonging, as familiar and unpretentious as the handwriting in your journal.*

So as you write in these pages, whatever it is you write—thoughts, feelings, notes from your life, words of sadness or wonderment—we trust you will find a certain companionship in the voices here, and perhaps inspiration as well. It has been said that "one who writes in a diary is never lonely," and it may be all the more true in this volume.

Writing in your journal, like practicing Earth prayer, can be a spiritual path. Both are an active form of receptivity. Both are enhanced by your capacity to feel deeply and to perceive vividly through your senses. Both require that you notice, appreciate, and embrace the world around you, joining your inner life with its rhythms. It is in this spirit that we have created Honoring the Earth: A Journal of New Earth Prayers, *recognizing that the personal act of writing in a journal helps awaken and stimulate these same internal capacities that nourish Earth prayer.*

Journaling as Recollection

You find a moment, you make a cup of tea, you sit down by yourself at a window seat, or in bed, or under a tree, and you open the journal, pausing to recollect where you have been and who you are becoming. It is as if between the covers of your journal you enter a place of spiritual retreat and contemplation, much as a nun or monk enters her or his simple cell. Here the rapid flow of daily business is left outside. In the private world of your journal a sense of spaciousness unfolds, held in focus by the thoughtful movement of your pen on the page.

It is just this combination of spaciousness and focus that is the essence of prayer. T. S. Eliot called it "concentration without elimination." While concentration normally narrows our focus, eliminating everything else from our field of vision, prayer—and especially Earth prayer—welcomes all of creation to be present in the same moment of focused attention.

Glance at the sun.

See the moon and the stars.

Gaze at the beauty of the earth's greenings.

Now,

Think.[2]

One-pointedness and wonderment, concentration and awe, this is the mindfulness of Earth prayer that can touch you as you keep this journal. You can recollect the world here, you can recollect yourself, bringing into focus your unbounded intuition. But beware that these wonderful possibilities don't burden you with self-conscious expectations. Remember this journal is above all your good friend, relaxed and nonjudgmental. In your honest presence it can awaken without force this gift of concentration and wonderment that is at the heart of all spiritual heritages.

Journaling as Observation

Amidst the speed and demands of modern life it is easy to become desensitized to the rich mysteries of the here *and* now. *In the process of protecting ourselves we contract, shutting down many of the receptive circuits that link us to our environment and to the individual beings that complete it. This contraction makes us feel isolated from the meaning of our lives. It is this contraction that the practice of spiritual journaling releases.*

Here's an exercise: if one day when you open your journal you feel at a loss for what to write or how to be, just start describing the immediate present. Write about the forms and colors you see, the sounds you hear, the smells of the place. With as much detail as you can, describe the moment as it unfolds, including your own unfolding feelings. Be the scribe of your senses. If you get lost, come back to the moment. This kind of journaling creates a lightning rod from body to spirit—as you record the intense cold, the howl of dogs, the silhouette of a mountain, the shades of green in fir trees, you attune to the immanence of the spirit in these things. When this happens you are part of the Earth praying, an unselfconscious witness, God's mirror:

> I offer my eyes to the Earth
> > So that it can have my perspective
> Offer all my senses
> > So that all that I see from this place
> > > The Earth can see [3]

Journaling as Blessing

The science of ecology is often described as the study of energy flows through living systems. A spiritual description of ecology might call these energy flows "currents in the great sea of blessing." The sun blesses the Earth with its warmth, the clouds bless the land with rain, the land blesses the seeds with nourishment, the plants bless the animals with food. Each breath we take is a blessing from the green leaves of our planet, and each breath we exhale is our blessing back to those leaves. In ways often invisible to the eye we touch and sustain one another.

And so it can be here in the private world of your journal. Though no one may ever read what you write on these pages, the intentions you express can align you with, deepen, and direct, these "currents of blessing" in which we all are immersed. Through our capacity for intention we become mindful cocreators in this unfolding Universe. "Have a good day!" we call after each other. "Take care!" "Happy birthday!" "Good luck!" We offer each other blessings all the time, and somehow alive beneath the secular nature of these invocations is our faith in their efficacy. Is this superstition or magic? No, it is our conscious participation in the creative flux of things, our intentional engagement with the primary law that everything we do affects the whole.

You may wish to explore writing some of these "prayers of intention." There are a number of common forms of blessings, invocations, praise, and thanksgiving, which you will find illustrated in this journal and in the book Earth Prayers. *Most often they begin with an invocatory phrase (which is often repeated) followed by a litany of variations. For example, note the repetition of the word* let *in this prayer:*

> Let my plant bring forth Thy flowers,
> Let my fruit produce Thy seed,
> Let my heart become Thy lute, Beloved,
> And my body Thy flute of reed.[4]

Here are a few other examples from which you may wish to create prayers:

> May *(the Earth continue to live. . .)*
> Peace *(to the plant and peace to the trees. . .)*
> Make *(my prayer sticks into something alive. . .)*
> Remember, remember *(the young within the nest. . .)*
> Bless *(our land and people. . .)*
> Blessed be *(these hands that have embraced with passion. . .)*
> Praise *(wet snow falling early. . .)*
> We return thanks *(to the rivers and streams. . .)*

Blessings like these radiate outward and inward at the same time, touching the one-who-prays and the prayed-for equally. As you write in this journal try using them. Create your own blessing ways. Deepen your powers of observation and presence. Recollect the world and yourself through concentration and wonder. You will feel connected to a lineage of Earth prayer that has come alive through all cultures and traditions, and your voice, however humbly, will carry that life onward in these pages.

---

1. Lee Henderson
2. Hildegard of Bingen
3. John Seed
4. Hazrat Inayat Khan

To feel and speak the astonishing beauty of things—
earth, stone and water,
Beast, man and woman, sun, moon and stars—

—Robinson Jeffers

The earth spirit has been laid down
It is covered over with the growing things,
It has been laid down
The earth is beautiful.

—*Navajo chant*

O burning mountain, O chosen sun,

O perfect moon, O fathomless well,

O unattainable height, O clearness beyond measure,

O wisdom without end, O mercy without limit,

O strength beyond resistance, O crown of all majesty,

The humblest you created sings your praise.

—*Mechthild of Magdeburg*

May we open to a deeper understanding
and a genuine love and caring
for the multitude of faces,
who are none other than ourself.

—*Wendy Egyoku Nakao*

O God of the mountains and valleys,
I have offered you a bit of your food, your drink.
And now I continue on, beneath your feet and your hands,
I, a traveler.

—*Kekchi Mayan song*

In God's wildness is the hope of the world—
the great fresh, unblighted, unredeemed wilderness.

—*John Muir*

Bless the streams and the mountains,
the trees, the grass, the shrubs,
Great Spirit, bless our Mother Earth
so our people may continue to live
in harmony with nature.

—*Pete Catches, Sr.*

❦

Our prayer of thanks

For the laughter of children who tumble barefooted
and bareheaded in the summer grass.

—*Carl Sandburg*

You pray in your distress
and in your need;
would that you might pray
also in the fullness of your joy
and in your days of abundance.

—*Kahlil Gibran*

ॐ

O Mother Gaia
sky   cloud   gate   milk   snow
wind-void-world
I bow in roadside gravel

—*Gary Snyder*

To bless whatever there is,
and for no other reason but simply because it is,
that is what we are made for as human beings.

—*David Steindl-Rast*

In one salutation to thee, my God,
let all my senses spread out
and touch this world at thy feet.

—*Rabindranath Tagore*

In God all that is, is God.
In Him the smallest creature
of the earth and sea
is worth no atom less
than you or me.

—*Angelus Silesius*

The river is smooth and calm this evening.

The Spring flowers bloom.

The moon floats on the current.

The tide carries the stars.

—*The Emperor Yang of Sui*

Since the whole world

Cannot buy

A single spring day,

Of what avail

To seek yellow gold?

—*Hsi Pei Lan*

I arise today

Through the strength of heaven:

Light of sun,

Radiance of moon,

Splendour of fire.

Speed of lightning,

Swiftness of wind,

Depth of sea,

Stability of earth,

Firmness of rock.

—*Saint Patrick*

Spring, and no one can be still,

with all the messages coming through.

—*Rumi*

What would become of our souls,
if they lacked the bread of earthly reality to nourish them,
the wine of created beauty to intoxicate them,
the discipline of human struggle to make them strong?

—*Pierre Teilhard de Chardin*

Newborn, on the naked sand

Nakedly lay it,

Next to the earth mother,

That it may know her;

Having good thoughts of her, the food giver.

—*Grande Pueblo song*

❦

As I kneel to put the seed in

careful as stitching, I am in love.

You are the bed we all sleep on.

You are the food we eat, the food

we ate, the food we will become.

We are walking trees rooted in you.

—*Marge Piercy*

Help us to be the always hopeful
Gardeners of the spirit
Who know that without darkness
Nothing comes to birth
As without light
Nothing flowers.

—*May Sarton*

Now may every living thing,
young or old, weak or strong,
living near or far, known or unknown,
living or departed or yet unborn,
may every living thing be full of bliss.

—*Buddha*

ॐ

Let there be peace in the sky
and in the atmosphere,
peace in the plant world and in the forests;
Let the cosmic powers be peaceful;
Let there be fulfilling peace everywhere.

—*Atharvaveda*

℘

Let us join the Great Mother,
Change blood into milk, clay into vessel,
egg into child, wind into song,
our bodies into worship.

—*Elizabeth Roberts*

Thou art blest among the planets

blest beneath the feet

of the dancing circle of women.

—*Lee Henderson*

The sky is filled with stars and the sun,
this earth with life vibrant.
Amongst it all I too have received a home
out of this wonder my song is born.

—*Rabindranath Tagore*

I got a home in dat rock,

Don't you see?

Between de earth an' sky,

Thought I heard my Saviour cry,

You got a home in dat rock,

Don't you see?

—*African-American spiritual*

The wild deer wandering here & there
Keeps the human soul from care.

—*William Blake*

May the gentleness of spring rains
soften the tensions within us,
And the power of ocean waves
steady and strengthen us.

—*Janet Schaffran and Pat Kozak*

☍

I am circling around God, around the ancient tower,
and I have been circling for a thousand years.
And I still don't know if I am a falcon
or a storm, or a great song.

—*Rainer Maria Rilke*

Slow me down, God, and inspire me to send

my roots deep

into the soil of life's enduring values

that I may grow toward the stars

and unfold my destiny.

—*Wilfred Peterson*

It may be that some little root of the sacred tree still lives.

Nourish it then, that it may leaf and bloom and fill with singing birds.

—Black Elk

Mother Earth.

It is you who feed us, shelter us, teach us, heal us.

And like unthinking children we squander your riches,

taking without thought for the future.

—*Judith Favia*

We can hear it in water, in wood, and even in stone.

We are earth of this earth, and we are bone of its bone.

This is a prayer I sing, for we have forgotten this and so

The earth is perishing.

—*Barbara Deming*

I hold sacred
the natural order of the earth
and vow to do my utmost
to help turn the tide
of our Earth's devastation.

—*Anonymous*

◌

I am ignorant, please have patience
and help me to learn. Show me how.
This is my prayer to the living Earth,
my humble request.

—*Robin Holder*

Let us plead with ourselves to live in a way
which will not deprive other living beings
of air, water, food, shelter,
or the chance to live.

—*Thich Nhat Hahn*

All you who will come after me on this Earth,

be with me now.

It is for your sakes, that I work to heal our world.

Help me to be faithful in the task that must be done

so that there will be for you, as there was for me,

blue sky, fruitful land, clear waters.

—*Joanna Macy*

It is taught we reap what we sow
No crime or compassion will go unpaid
The earth's harvest of tears we have seeded
So her healing, in our hands, God has laid

—*Maureen Curle*

For all these years
you've protected
the seed.
It's time to become
the flower.

—*Stephen C. Paul*

We are all children of the one God.

God is listening to me.
The sun, the darkness, the winds,
are all listening to what we now say.

—*Geronimo*

❧

We belong to the ground
It is our power
And we must stay close to it
or maybe we will get lost.

—*Narritjin Maymuru Yirrkala*

My ceiling the sky, my carpet the grass,

My music the lowing of herds as they pass;

My books are the brooks, my sermons the stones,

My parson's a wolf on a pulpit of bones.

—*Allen McCanless*

one old man sitting alone

perched in these green mountains

a small shack   the retired life   letting my hair grow white

pleased with the years gone by   happy with today

mindless this life is like water flowing east

—Han-Shan

May every living being, seen and unseen

Those dwelling far-off, those near-by

Those already born, those waiting to be born

May all attain inward peace.

—*The Sutta Nipata*

Glance at the sun.

See the moon and the stars.

Gaze at the beauty of earth's greenings.

Now,

Think.

—*Hildegard of Bingen*

May the Great Spirit
watch over you

As long as the grass grows
and the water flows

—*Cherokee song*

The moon in the pines
Now I hang it up, now I take it off
And still I keep gazing.

—*Haiku*

In the empty mountains
I see no one,
But hear the sound
Of someone's voice.

—*Wang Wei*

Something opens our wings.

Something makes boredom and hurt disappear.

Someone fills the cup in front of us:

We taste only sacredness.

—*Rumi*

࿇

Coming, going, the waterfowl
Leaves not a trace,
Nor does it need a guide.

—Dogen

I'm so grateful to be alone:
crickets in darkening grass
a walk among pine trees
be with the ocean's pulse
or the silent early dawn.

—*Svein Myreng*

I know myself
alone.
The quiet places,
moss and stone,
are mine,
the breathing hills.

—*Nancy Rose Exeter*

For the person with attention,

every day

becomes the very day

upon which all the world depends.

—*Rami M. Shapiro*

∞

Watching the moon
at dawn,
solitary, mid-sky,
I knew myself completely:
no part left out.

—*Izumi Shikibu*

The sun and stars that float in the open air,
The apple-shaped earth and we upon it, surely the drift
of them is something grand.

—*Walt Whitman*

Like the cry of watchful birds swimming in water,

like the loud claps of thundering rain-clouds,

like joyful streams gushing from the mountain,

so have our hymns sounded forth to the Lord.

—*The Rig Veda*

❦

I have clothed myself in riches

Sewn by hands in praise of home

I am made of pollen and wings and bone

I am wind reflected in moonlight

I am ice crying out for flood

I am fields released by rain

I give to you this life

Claimed by what I do not own.

—*Nancy Wood*

I offer my eyes to the Earth

So that it can have my perspective

Offer all my senses

So that all that I see from this place

The Earth can see

—John Seed

Let my plant bring forth Thy flowers,

Let my fruit produce Thy seed,

Let my heart become Thy lute, Beloved,

And my body Thy flute of reed.

—*Hazrat Inayat Khan*

O wild earth, bless my loneliness
with your solitude.
Answer my longing
with your silence.

—*Elias Amidon*

𝒮

When the wind blows, that is my medicine

When it rains, that is my medicine

When it hails, that is my medicine

When it becomes clear after a storm,

that is my medicine.

—Wolf Coller

Ocean Spirit

calm the waves for me

get close to me, my power

my heart is tired

make the sea like milk for me

yeho

yeholo

—Haida song

Night is drawing nigh

For all that has been—Thanks!

For all that shall be—Yes!

—Dag Hammarskjöld

Every day is a renewal,

every morning the daily miracle.

This joy you feel is life.

—*Gertrude Stein*

We give thanks for sun and moon,

dark night and day, rain and clouds,

fertile field and sky, springtime and harvest,

growth and rest.

—*Congregation of Abraxas*

How infinite are your creatures, Unnameable One!

With wisdom you made them all.

The whole earth is filled with your riches.

—Psalm 104

Pray for the animals, you that pray,
you that beg for mercy, for success and for peace,
the immanent spirit has also been poured unto them,
they are also souls, more complete than you,
and clear, brave, beautiful.

—*Eeva-Liisa Manner*

I pledge allegiance to this earth,
and all the peoples on it; and to the
ocean which surrounds us all; all creatures,
all beings, the sky above—
with understanding and compassion for all.

—*Adrienne Skyborne*

kind be the wind

calm the sea

may all the elements

benevolent agree

to your desire

—Anonymous

The waters of the sky or those that flow, those that are
dug out or those that arise by themselves, those pure
and clear waters that seek the ocean as their goal—
let the waters, who are goddesses, help me here and now.

—*The Rig Veda*

❦

I love it tree because e love me too.

E watching me same as you

tree e working with your body, my body,

e working with us.

While you sleep e working.

Daylight, when you walking around, e work too.

—*Bill Neidjie*

The earth is looking at me; she is looking up at me

I am looking down on her

I am happy, she is looking at me

I am happy, I am looking at her.

—*Navajo chant*

The moon's the same old moon,
The flowers exactly as they were,
Yet I've become the thingness
Of all the things I see!

—*Bunan*

We are all the children of. . .

A brilliantly colored flower,

A flaming flower.

And there is no one,

There is no one

Who regrets what we are.

—*Ramón Medina Silva*

In you, in this plant,
resides the Mother goddess
and when I water you
when I return nurturance to you
I am returning nurturance
to the Mother goddess
who supports this world.

—*Song from India*

My heart was split, and a flower
appeared; and grace sprang up;
and it bore fruit for my God.

—*The Odes of Solomon*

To be like these, straight, true and fine,

To make our world, like theirs, a shrine;

Sink down, O, traveller, on your knees,

God stands before you in these trees.

—*Joseph B. Strause*

Almighty One, in the woods I am blessed.

Happy everyone in the woods.

Every tree speaks through thee. O God!

What glory in the woodland!

—*Ludwig van Beethoven*

May the axe be far away from you;

May the fire be far away from you;

May there be rain without storm;

Lord of Trees, may you be blessed;

Lord of Trees, may I be blessed.

—*Hindu prayer*

Because you can die of overwork, because

you can die of the fire that melts

rock, because you can die of the poison

that kills the beetle and the slug,

we must come again to worship you

on our knees, the common living dirt.

—*Marge Piercy*

↬

My gentle hill, I rest
beside you in the dark
in a place warmed by my body,
where by ardor, grace, work,
and loss, I belong.

—*Wendell Berry*

ರ೦

God, I have sought you as a fox seeks chickens,

curbing my hunger with cunning.

The times I have tasted your flesh

there was no bread and wine between us,

only night and the wind beating the grass.

—*Alden Nowlan*

Sunsets and rainbows, green forest and restive blue seas, all
naturally colored things are my siblings. We have played
together on the floor of the world
Since the first stone looked up
At the stars.

—*Maya Angelou*

Touch the earth and listen to the rocks

for they remember

They know and remember

all that has come to pass here.

—*Lee Henderson*

❧

And forget not that the earth delights to feel your bare feet and the winds long to play with your hair.

—*Kahlil Gibran*

Living in a forest
I am wrapt round by goddesses.
Lifting their arms and their hair
they spin soft green whispers,
speaking to each other
and to me in the morning.

—*Carol Atkins*

God of all creation,

grant us this day

some meeting with bird or moon,

sheep or star, insect or the sun itself:

that we might marvel and know our place

and praise you again and for ever and ever.

—*Gabe Huck*

I prayed for humility and I saw a mountain towering above me.

I prayed to know the truth and I heard the stream.

I prayed for a blessing and I felt a single raindrop.

I prayed for pleasure and I felt my body come alive.

—*John Davis*

Every bird song, wind song, and

tremendous storm song of the rocks

in the heart of the mountains is our song,

our very own, and sings our love.

—*John Muir*

Will we let the wind sing to us?

Do our whole bodies listen?

When the wind calls, will we go?

—*Susan Griffin*

The voice of my fathers is on the wind
and my voice also when it becomes strong
for only my sons to hear and keep on
hearing after I am gone.

—*Nancy Wood*

Blessed among all weather is
the snowfall, that by crowding the
air reveals it, and by covering the
earth discloses it: definer of
surfaces, angel of edges, bringer of
peace.

—*Catherine Madsen*

May he who brings

flowers tonight

have moonlight.

—*Kikaku*

Don't pray for the rain to stop.
Pray for good luck fishing
when the river floods.

—*Wendell Berry*

Naked you came from Earth the Mother.

Naked you return to her.

May a good wind be your road.

—Omaha song

I add my breath to your breath

that our days may be long on the Earth,

that the days of our people may be long,

that we shall be as one person,

that we may finish our road together.

—*Laguna Pueblo song*

Beauty crowds me till I die

Beauty mercy have on me

But if I expire today

Let it be in sight of thee—

—*Emily Dickinson*

I pray

To dissolve myself in the Earth

To feel humanness dissolve back into the

Earth

Whence it came

—*John Seed*

Here lays
a small dead squirrel
ready to become
a Rose

—*Bruce Ho*

In the next world, should I remember
this one, I will praise it
above everything.

—*David Ignatow*

There is a blessedness surely to be believed,
and that is that everything abides in
eternal ecstasy, now and forever.

—*Jack Kerouac*

To fling my arms wide

In some place of the sun,

To whirl and to dance

Till the white day is done.

Then rest at cool evening

Beneath a tall tree

While night comes on gently,

Dark like me—

That is my dream!

—Langston Hughes

For sixty years I have been forgetful,

every minute, but not for a second

has this flowing toward me stopped or slowed.

—*Rumi*

If the only prayer you say in your entire life is "Thank you," that would suffice.

—*Meister Eckhart*

ACKNOWLEDGMENTS

Grateful acknowledgment is made to the following for permission to reprint material copyrighted or controlled by them:

For Maya Angelou: from *Now Sheba Sings the Song,* copyright © 1987 by Maya Angelou. Used by permission of Dial Books for Young Readers, a division of Penguin Books, USA, Inc.

For Wendell Berry: from "Prayers and Sayings of the Mad Farmer" in *Farming: A Handbook,* copyright © 1970 by Wendell Berry. Reprinted by permission of Harcourt Brace & Company; from "Song(2)" in *Collected Poems 1957–1982* by Wendell Berry, copyright © 1982, 1984 by Wendell Berry. Reprinted by permission of North Point Press, a division of Farrar, Straus & Giroux, Inc.

For Bunan and Dogen: from *Zen Poems of China* by Lucien Stryk, Takashi Ikemoto, and Taigan Takayama, copyright © 1973 by Lucien Stryk, Takayashi Ikemoto, and Taigan Takayama. Used by permission of Doubleday, a division of Bantam Doubleday Dell Publishing Group, Inc.

For Pete Catches, Sr.: from *Meditations with Native Americans* by Paul Steinmetz, copyright © 1984, Bear & Co., Inc., P.O. Drawer 2860, Santa Fe, NM 87504.